W9-DJH-450

Smelly Old History

GREEK GRIME

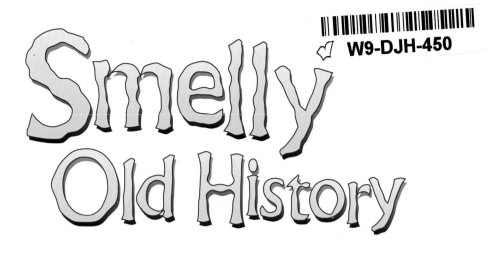

Mary Dobson

OXFORD UNIVERSITY PRESS

Oxford University Press, Great Clarendon Street, Oxford OX2 6DP

Oxford New York
Athens Auckland Bangkok Bogotá Bombay
Buenos Aires Calcutta Cape Town Dar es Salaam
Delhi Florence Hong Kong Istanbul Karachi
Kuala Lumpur Madras Madrid Melbourne
Mexico City Nairobi Paris Singapore
Taipei Tokyo Toronto Warsaw

and associated companies in
Berlin Ibadan

Oxford is a trade mark of Oxford University Press

© Mary Dobson 1998
First published 1998

Artwork: Vince Reid. Photographs: British Museum, London: 5br,16;
Ashmolean Museum, Oxford: 17; The American School of Classical Studies, Athens: 5bl.

All rights reserved. No part of this publication may be reproduced,
stored in a retrieval system, or transmitted, in any form or by any means,
without the prior permission in writing of Oxford University Press.
Within the UK, exceptions are allowed in respect of any fair dealing for the
purpose of research or private study, or criticism or review, as permitted
under the Copyright, Designs, and Patents Act, 1988, or in the case of
reprographic reproduction in accordance with the terms of the licences
issued by the Copyright Licensing Agency. Enquiries concerning
reproduction outside those terms and in other countries should be
sent to the Rights Department, Oxford University Press,
at the address above.

This book is sold subject to the condition that it shall not, by way
of trade or otherwise, be lent, re-sold, hired out or otherwise circulated
without the publisher's prior consent in any form of binding or cover
other than that in which it is published and without similar condition
including this condition being imposed on the subsequent purchaser.

A CIP catalogue record for this book is available from the British Library

ISBN 0-19-910493-X

1 3 5 7 9 10 8 6 4 2

Printed in Great Britain

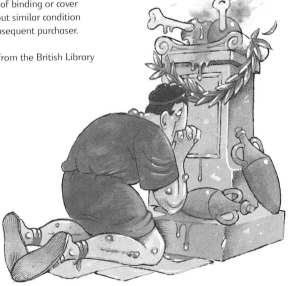

CONTENTS

Scratch the scented panels lightly with a
fingernail to release their smell.

A SENSE OF THE PAST

The ancient Greek way of life was a model of purity and perfection. Athletes and heroes kept their bodies in beautiful shape. But that meant removing all the grime and sweat, and pouring on the oils.

Of all the senses of the past, we often forget the sense of smell! This book brings you up to scratch with the odours of ancient grease. Sniff out a few fragrant facts, or turn up your nose at some foul ones.

The ancient Greek civilisation spans 3000 years, from about 3200 BC to 30 BC. It began with the Minoans in Crete and the Mycenaeans in Greece. These ancients even enjoyed flushing toilets. The next era was more grimy, and not really civilised. In the 8th century the poet Homer began telling tales of mythical monsters and handsome heroes – these may have been pure myth, but they do tell us just how smelly old history could be. The golden age of ancient Greece lasted from 480 BC to 323 BC. This was the era of classical grease! Greek grime spread far and wide, until the last century BC when the rotten Romans took over.

Sweaty Greeks invaded Troy hidden in a wooden horse

4

GREEK GRIME

The olive tree grew far and wide
In ancient Greece, it was their pride.
What mattered most in war and peace
Was keeping pure with ancient grease.

It all began with Athena's tree,
A gift to Zeus with the power to be
The sacred symbol of ancient Greeks,
The essential oil for smelly reeks.

Now just imagine if you had been
A potty Greek all sparkling clean.
How would you deal with sweat and toil,
And keep your body drenched in oil?

At first you take off dirt and grime,
And then you pick out spots and slime.
Your strigil proves an ideal stick -
A few good scrapes will do the trick.

And then it's time to fill your nose
With perfumed oils of fragrant rose.
Your slave rubs down your skin and hair -
The perfect greasy body care!

Imagine now a pungent thought:
You've just enjoyed a spot of sport,
You soon begin to scratch and sniff,
Your glistening body starts to whiff.

You rush back to the changing place
Before your odours cause disgrace.
But now, to your immense dismay,
A robber's whipped your stuff away!

To lose a toga's not too sad,
But life without your oils is bad!
So bring back pots of ancient time
To revive the smell of old Greek grime.

Greek babies had clay
potties for their needs.

**These feet of
clay held
fragrant oils**

ANCIENT GREASE

The Minoan civilisation sprang up on the island of Crete around 3000 BC. The Minoans were pure and peaceful, and their rulers lived in amazing palaces. They had bathrooms, decent drains, and even the first flushing toilets in the world!

The queen's chamber in the palace at Knossos.

According to a legend, King Minos of Crete sacrificed fourteen young Athenians to a monstrous minotaur who lived in a labyrinth. Finally, the Athenian hero, Theseus, slew the minotaur. There may even be a whiff of truth in the story - these amazing drains under the King's Palace look just like the minotaur's maze!

The Mycenaeans, who lived on mainland Greece, were another great civilisation. They enjoyed fighting, and their warriors wore helmets made with rows of boars' tusks. They also loved rich scents and golden objects. Mycenaean kings were wrapped in gold foil when they were buried.

Mycenaean perfume makers hard at work in their workshop in 1300 BC. Violets were everybody's favourite.

Scratch and sniff this very ancient aroma.

By 1200 BC these fragrant civilisations had gone down the drain. No-one quite knows what went wrong, but we do know that flushing toilets didn't reappear on the scene for another 3000 years.

GREEK REEKS

You've probably heard of the Trojan horse, but have you ever wondered what it must have smelt like inside? Follow the story from Homer's famous poems, *The Iliad* and *The Odyssey*.

Beautiful Helen of Sparta is married to Menelaus, the brother of King Agamemnon of Mycenae. Menelaus smells of horse manure and sweaty armour, which doesn't appeal to Helen.

Paris, a prince from Troy, plans to capture Helen. Aphrodite, the goddess of love, sends him the secret of scent. His amorous aroma is sensational! Helen loves Paris's perfume and nips off to Troy with him.

Mouldy old Menelaus isn't too pleased, and he gets his brother Agamemnon to send an army and a thousand ships to Troy. No luck - ten years later, Paris is dead but the Greeks still haven't managed to get into the city.

Then the Greeks come up with a brilliant idea! They build a massive wooden horse, leave it outside the gates of Troy as a present, and pretend to sail away.

The Trojans are naturally nosy, and wheel the gift into the city. But they don't have the sense to poke their noses inside - and just as well, because cooped up in the hollow horse are lots of sweaty soldiers. Odysseus is in control, but his warriors are crossing their legs hoping the Trojans won't sniff them out.

The Greeks can't hold on much longer. During the night they spill out, and open the gates of Troy to let in the rest of King Agamemnon's army. Troy falls, and Helen has to go back to her smelly old husband.

ODOROUS LABOURS

Making sense of Greek gods and monsters, mortals and immortals can be a bit of a struggle. Try to wrap your mind around this story, to get the full flavour!

Zeus, king of the gods, is married to his sister, Hera. Zeus has lots of children including a mortal son, Heracles. This drives the immortal Hera mad. Eventually, she drives Heracles mad, and he murders his wife and children. Horrified, Heracles asks the gods to forgive him. He is told to perform twelve 'impossible tasks' set by King Eurystheus. Heracles does the impossible . . . and so becomes immortal!

The first of the Twelve Labours is unbelievably tough. Heracles must kill the Nemean lion, which lives in a cave with a sickening stench. Its skin is too thick to be pierced by a weapon. No sweat! Heracles holds his breath and strangles it with his bare hands.

The king hopes Heracles will foul up the second labour, in the reeking swamps of Lerna. The wise goddess Athene warns Heracles of the deadly smell of the nine-headed water monster, Hydra. But Heracles overcomes this odorous labour and, before long, the monster's completely de-hydra-ted!

Heracles could have mucked up the fifth task! Eurystheus tells him to clean out the stables of King Augeus in one day. These are overflowing with the foulest, filthiest piles of manure in the kingdom. Heracles is very smart - he has no intention of wallowing in piles of dung. He simply diverts two rivers to do his dirty work.

To prove your Heraclean strength, scratch and sniff this horsey whiff.

11

SIZZLING SACRIFICES

The Greeks worshipped many gods and goddesses. They believed they lived like one big happy family on Mount Olympos. But they could turn nasty. To prevent them being rotten to you, it was essential to stay pure.

Poor old Spotticus is in a bad way. He hasn't spent enough time washing his body and soul. Zeus's twins, Apollo and Artemis, have inflicted some nasty boils on him.

Perhaps a nice little sizzling sacrifice will cure him. Greasy thigh bones make a delicious offering, but it's a bit smelly for the twins. So Spotticus pours on lots of incense, and sends them prayers and promises with sweet-smelling smoke.

This doesn't do the trick, so Spotticus pops off to the Temple at Epidauros, where the spicy smell of burning laurel is overpowering. He falls into a deep sleep and dreams that Hygieia, daughter of Asclepius, the great god of medicine, is giving him some extra-strong oils to pop his boils. She tells him to take more baths in future. In gratitude for this hygienic advice, Spotticus leaves behind two model boils.

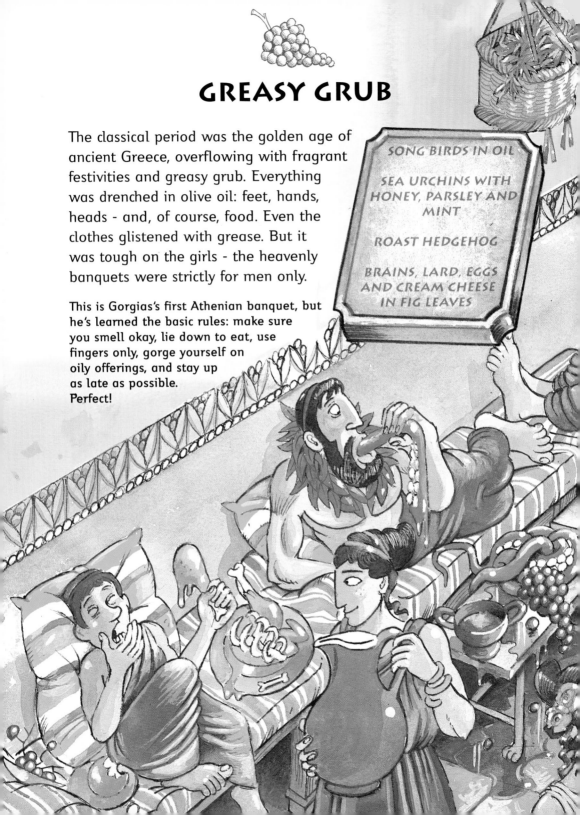

GREASY GRUB

The classical period was the golden age of ancient Greece, overflowing with fragrant festivities and greasy grub. Everything was drenched in olive oil: feet, hands, heads - and, of course, food. Even the clothes glistened with grease. But it was tough on the girls - the heavenly banquets were strictly for men only.

This is Gorgias's first Athenian banquet, but he's learned the basic rules: make sure you smell okay, lie down to eat, use fingers only, gorge yourself on oily offerings, and stay up as late as possible. Perfect!

SONG BIRDS IN OIL

SEA URCHINS WITH HONEY, PARSLEY AND MINT

ROAST HEDGEHOG

BRAINS, LARD, EGGS AND CREAM CHEESE IN FIG LEAVES

Tedius is being a real bore, stuffing his head with a grave Greek text called *Concerning Odours* by Theophrastus. But it does list all the essential oils you could ever want, and even tells you how to deal with obnoxious odours.

Scratch and sniff Tedius's floral wreath to find out what's on his mind.

A slave purifies a late arrival. Tereus is just in time for the dancing girls, pan pipes and poetry. He takes a gulp of wine to get in the party mood. Ugh! It's been stored in a pig's bladder.

AROMATIC ATHLETICS

Ancient Greek boys spent the best part of their lives keeping fit - and the rest keeping fragrant!

Oileus and Ajax can barely wait for the gymnasium. Did you know the word 'gymnasium' means 'an exercise for which you strip'? And in ancient Greece, it's essential to strip off all the grime, as well as your clothes, before exercising. Ajax scrapes off his grime with a strigil. The slave collects the grime in a pot: this stuff was actually used as a magical ointment for skin diseases! Oileus grabs the oil. He needn't worry - there's at least a pint for them both!

Strigils and an oil flask.

Their oily skins feel beautifully supple as they challenge each other to the diskos and javelin. After a while, Ajax tells his friend his armpits smell like a goat's. It's back to the bathroom!

They round off the day with a wrestling match. Oileus wallows in the mud to make his body even more slippery. Ajax can hardly grab hold of him. He tries a sneaky trick, and sticks his finger up Oileus' nose. But the trainer's on to him with the rules: no gouging an opponent's eyes, nose or mouth, and no biting. This wrestling scene is painted on a real Greek vase.

OILY OLYMPICS

Aromatic athletics were carried to dizzy heights at the great Olympic festival, held in honour of the god Zeus. This exciting event first took place in 776 BC, and then every four years. It lasted five days. All the best athletes from miles around gathered at Olympia, and crowds of spectators poured in to watch. Nike, the goddess of victory, kept the athletes on their toes, but the only prizes were wreaths from the sacred olive tree near by.

The athletes are wearing nothing but olive oil! No-one quite knows when this fashion started. According to one story, at the Olympics in 720 BC one athlete was so greasy that his shorts fell off in the middle of a race, but he still went on to win. After that no-one saw the point of trying to hang on to their clothes.

This runner is already flat-out and the race hasn't even started yet.

100 oxen have just been sacrificed at the Temple of Zeus.

Women aren't allowed to compete - they can be thrown off the nearest cliff if spotted.

GRUESOME GREEKS

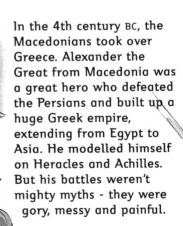

From the 8th century BC, ancient Greece was divided into a number of city states, each with its own government. They fought gruesome battles against each other, but occasionally they banded together to fight a foreign enemy.

Athens and Sparta were bitter rivals. Sparta had a full-time army. Boys from the age of seven were trained to fight in harsh conditions - so they quickly learnt to keep cool.

The Scythians were a nomadic tribe from the Russian Steppes. They were the enemies of the Spartans. But both had strange customs. A Scythian soldier drank the blood of the first man he killed. A Spartan spent hours oiling his body and combing his hair before a battle!

In the 4th century BC, the Macedonians took over Greece. Alexander the Great from Macedonia was a great hero who defeated the Persians and built up a huge Greek empire, extending from Egypt to Asia. He modelled himself on Heracles and Achilles. But his battles weren't mighty myths - they were gory, messy and painful.

In 490 BC the Athenians beat the Persians at the battle of Marathon. Pheidippides ran a marathon to Athens with the news. To retaliate, the Persians then destroyed Athens. But the Greeks got their own back in a bloody sea battle.

BACK TO BASICS

Imagine living in late 5th-century BC Athens. It's a magnificent, democratic city which has just been rebuilt by its great leader, Pericles. The crowning glory is the Parthenon - a glorious temple to Athena perched high on the Acropolis.

The rich live in large houses with open courtyards and lavish lavatories, but the poor are crammed into tight little corners. Poor Nicias can't even find room for her waste.

The central area, the Agora, is thronged with the fragrant odours of food and flowers - and donkeys!

A LIFE OF GRIME

One of the darker sides of Greek life was slavery. Follow the miserable story of Carion.

Carion is a weak little scrap. His mum and dad abandon him soon after birth. But Prodicus the slave rearer makes a grab for him - he knows the value of a pound of flesh!

Carion is given lots of oily food to eat and grows up strong and fit - for a life in the silver mines. He works a 10-hour shift with 20,000 other slaves in the smelly, suffocating mines. He becomes filthy. His owner becomes filthy rich. There's only one way out: Carion decides to run away.

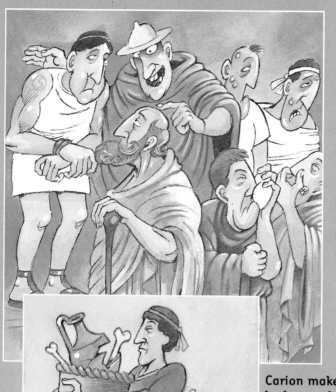

He's soon caught, branded and taken to market to be sold. He holds his breath waiting for someone to buy him. He knows that any slave with bad breath is a rotten deal. He's in luck! Hyperbolus, a wealthy Athenian philosopher, buys him for 80 drachmas.

Carion makes a fresh start. All he has to do for the rest of his slave labour is look after his mistress, clean the house and take young Telephus to school.

He can even take control when Telephus gets into a spot of trouble with his teacher at school.

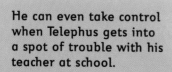

GRAVE GREEKS

There were many grave sides to Greek life - and death.

GRAVE SCHOLARS
During the golden age of Greek history, grave scholars turned their minds to weighty matters. For example, Archimedes noticed that when he got in the bath it overflowed. Then, Eureka! He realised he wasn't just wasting water, he was displacing it! And the amount was exactly equal to the volume of his body.

GRAVE DISEASES
In 430 BC a terrible plague killed a third of the population of Athens. Victims, including Pericles, reeled in agony and the stench of their boils was appalling. Burning sulphur was used to purify the city.

Scratch and sniff for a dreadful whiff!

GRAVE DOCTORS
A Greek doctor called Hippocrates had a strong influence on medicine for centuries. He said it wasn't just the gods that caused disease - it was bad smells! He had an old solution for his new theory of pollution: more baths and air fresheners.

GRAVE LAWS

One Greek politician, Solon, banned the sale of perfumes to men in Athens. Then he imposed the penalty of death on anyone who stole clothes and oil from the gymnasium. Trying to smell sweet became a grave issue.

GRAVE STINGS

Greeks kept bees for their pure sweet honey. They used burning cow dung to lure wild bees into an apiary. The bees were said to be disgusted by the smell of nasty Greeks and stung savagely.

GOING TO THE GRAVE

Ancient Greek funerals were elaborate. The body was washed, dressed and oiled, and sweet-smelling incense was burnt. The poor soul had to pay the boatman, Charon, to take him across the River Styx to the underworld called Hades. A foul soul went to Tartarus to be tortured. A pure one went to the fragrant Elysian Fields.

27

ROTTEN COMPETITION

In the 4th century BC, the Greeks were a mighty superpower. From then on, however, things began to go downhill.

In 323 BC Alexander the Great was overpowered by a stinking fever. The Greeks thought that foul swamps caused fevers, and in a way they were right - Alexander died of malaria, caused by a bite from a mosquito which breeds in swamps. Some people have blamed malaria for the fall of classical civilisation.

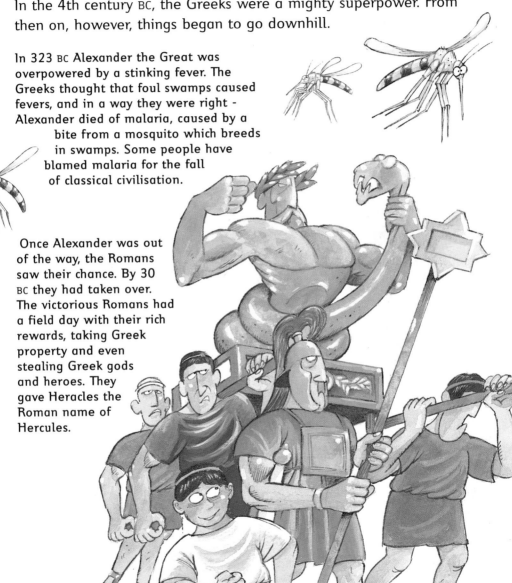

Once Alexander was out of the way, the Romans saw their chance. By 30 BC they had taken over. The victorious Romans had a field day with their rich rewards, taking Greek property and even stealing Greek gods and heroes. They gave Heracles the Roman name of Hercules.

The Olympic
Games became
fiercely competitive under
Roman rule. The rotten Romans
cheated and bribed the judges.
Their wrestling and boxing were
horribly brutal. But there was one
grimy Greek habit which they
found revolting: naked athletics.
They covered up for their combat.

The ancient Olympic
Games were finally
abandoned in
AD 393. But like
many bits of Greek
civilisation, they were dug up
again in the late 19th century.
The first modern Olympics were
held at Athens in 1896.

PUNGENT PUZZLES

Greek scientists and thinkers had many smelly problems to solve. Have a go at these stinkers yourself.

Aristotle tried to work out where lice and nits come from. He thought lice popped up naturally from rotting flesh, and that nits were their lousy offspring. What do you think?

The scientist Galen believed we smell with our brain, not with our nose! Does this make sense?

Plato argued there were only two sorts of smell: good and bad. How many can you come up with?

Pythagoras had a big problem with beans. He believed it was a bad idea to eat them, and he refused to let his followers even smell them. Modern science has found that some people have genes which protect them against malaria, but also make them sick if they eat beans. How do you think Pythagoras tried to sniff out the reason for this?

GLOSSARY

BC	Before Christ. Used to describe the years before the date of Christ's birth. The ancient Greeks would not have used this term.
city state	An area with its own city and government.
Elysian Fields	In Greek mythology, a pleasant part of the underworld.
gymnasium	A room where athletes exercised.
Hades	In Greek mythology, an unpleasant part of the underworld.
incense	A substance that gives off a pleasant smell when burned.
labyrinth	An underground maze.
malaria	A disease spread by mosquitoes.
Minoans	The people who lived in Crete 3000-1100 BC.
minotaur	In Greek mythology, a monster with a man's body and a bull's head.
Mount Olympos	The highest mountain in Greece. In Greek mythology, the home of the gods.
Mycenaeans	The people who lived in Greece 1600-1200 BC.
Olympic Games	Athletic games held every four years at Olympia.
pan pipes	A musical instrument made from reeds.
Parthenon	The temple dedicated to Athena, on the Acropolis in Athens.
philosopher	A scholar, from the Greek meaning 'lover of knowledge'.
strigil	An instrument for scraping oil and dirt off the skin.
Tartarus	In Greek mythology, the worst part of the underworld.

INDEX